Birds

BIRDS

Birds in the
ANIMAL
WORLD

Every detail of the skeleton of this Archaeopteryx has been preserved in soft limestone. The imprints of the teeth and feathers are clearly visible.

In search of the first bird

Whilst some groups within the animal kingdom present highly disparate features, birds are all strikingly similar to one other. Their biological make-up, from the very smallest hummingbird to the largest ostrich, is virtually identical.

Despite its brightly coloured plumage, the male European oriole is difficult to spot, so adept is it at camouflaging itself in the foliage at the tops of trees.

N ot many animals have succeeded in conquering the skies: a few mammals (bats), still fewer reptiles (some now-extinct dinosaurs) and a number of insects can, or could, all fly, but none of them can compete with birds for sheer aerial virtuosity. It is thanks to their capacity for flight that birds can be found all over the globe. There are birds in the skies over the coldest reaches of the North and South poles and over the hottest deserts. They can be found in the most temperate climates and over the vastest oceans. Yet their origins have long remained a mystery.

The peacock sets off the brilliant blue of its neck by fanning out its tail feathers.

Fossils found in South America have enabled scientists to reconstruct a Phororhacos. This remote ancestor of the crane was a swift runner and formidable carnivore.

Despite their size, pelicans are able to fly because their bones are hollow and this greatly reduces the body weight that they have to carry.

Nowadays, all that remains of the Aepyornis is its skeleton.

Archaeopteryx and Darwin's theory of evolution

Charles Darwin's *On the Origin of Species* (1859) shocked the scientific community of the time. It outlined a new theory of how the living world had developed, and contradicted the creationist theories that had held sway until then. Darwin established a relationship between different species and suggested that living species actually changed, or evolved, over time.

Aside from birds, few creatures are capable of proper flight, which requires a very small light body. The exceptions include bats and some insects.

▼ It is the possession of feathers that distinguishes an animal as belonging to the group classed as birds. The first role played by these appendages was probably that of insulation — a means of conserving body heat. Thanks to this natural overcoat, birds were able to withstand the cold, whereas reptiles were forced to find warm shelter. Feathers differ according to their function; wings, for example, are covered by remiges, stiff, light, aerodynamic feathers that enable the bird to stay aloft.

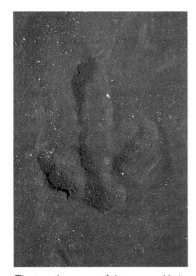

The two short toes of the emu enable it to run more easily.

The year 1860 saw the beginning of a period of discovery in the limestone quarries of the Solnhofen region in Bavaria. Here, fossils of a feathered animal were found that palaeontologists christened Archaeopteryx (from the Greek *archeo* 'old', and *pterux* 'feather'). Scientists were baffled by this prehistoric creature that had lived more than 140 million years ago because it appeared to combine the characteristics of both dinosaurs and birds. Darwin immediately saw this as further proof of his theory; the hybrid characteristics of Archaeopteryx did seem to indicate that birds developed as a distinct group from reptiles.

Teeth, feathers and claws

The fineness of the limestone at Solnhofen meant that every last detail of Archaeopteryx's remains had been perfectly preserved. Thus, from the moment when the very first fossil was discovered, the imprints of feathers in the limestone left no doubt that the creature in question was indeed a bird. Curiously, however, the upper and lower mandibles of the bird were lined with teeth, and its front limbs, transformed into wings, boasted three long fingers with claws. These strange

Birds such as the Australian emu have indentations along the beak but, unlike some of their ancestors, birds today do not have any teeth.

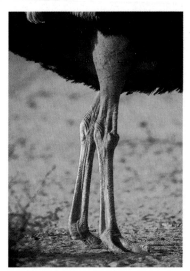

The ostrich has only two toes, whereas early birds had three or more.

characteristics led scientists to conclude that Archaeopteryx had developed from a group of small tree-dwelling dinosaurs.

Not yet equipped for flight

A primitive bird, Archaeopteryx's physique was not well adapted to flight. However, the asymmetrical form of its body and the aerodynamic outline of its wings must have enabled it at least to glide, if not actually fly properly in the way that modern birds do.

The wings of young crested hoatzins end in two clawed toes.
These 'primitive' appendages allow the birds to climb up trees soon after they hatch.

A long neck allows the emu to spot danger from a distance. Rather like an early-warning system, the sight of emus fleeing alerts other birds to the threat.

A difficult take-off

Archaeopteryx's ancestors, being even more cumbersome in the air, are thought to have made their first attempts at flight in one of two possible ways. The first hypothesis is that they were land birds that ran and jumped to capture their prey. According to this theory, they then developed stiff aerodynamic feathers (the first remiges) and some form of flight resulted from them beating their front limbs to propel themselves forward and to steady themselves as they landed.

For the pheasant, taking off is a long and arduous operation.

Aepyornis maximus (left) lived in Madagascar and *Megalapteryx didinus* in New Zealand. These birds had no predators until the arrival of settlers.

From a jump to a glide

The second hypothesis is that the early ancestors of birds climbed trees with the aid of their claws, then jumped off, using their wings to glide towards the next perch. This theory, which calls to mind the pitiful attempts at flight of our modern-day domestic chickens, seems the most likely of the two as it not only presents similarities between the bird and its ancestor the dinosaur, but also introduces the existence of claws similar to those of Archaeopteryx.

A razorbill takes advantage of a gust of wind to launch itself from the cliff.

The domestic cock struts proudly around the farmyard. Its small wings mean that it is incapable of flying long distances.

Herring gulls often fly in groups. They glide on air currents, scanning the ground in search of food.

A bar-headed goose has been spotted at an altitude of more than 8,000 metres.

Different skills, different behaviour

Despite the biological similarities between different types of birds, each species possesses particular skills that influence the way in which it lives. Thus birds of prey, armed with a sharp beak and claws, feed on the flesh of other animals whilst strong fliers cross the oceans or undertake extensive migratory journeys. Birds more at home sitting on a perch spend most of their time among trees whilst others, unable to fly, have learned to run, swim or dive in order to survive.

The arctic tern, a bird capable of covering huge distances, nests during the summer months in the high regions of the northern hemisphere.

Long-distance travellers

In developing the ability to move through the air, birds have acquired an extraordinary freedom — that of moving rapidly from place to place, unhampered by such obstacles as oceans, mountains and deserts that stand in the way of their earth-bound cousins.

Canada geese migrate from the north of the United States to the south. During such migrations they are often seen flying in a V formation.

M any birds make endless short journeys between their nest and the places where they hunt for food. In addition to this, some birds periodically undertake perilous migrations across extremely long distances. These large seasonal movements of the bird population usually take place when climatic conditions make it impossible for the birds to find food in one particular place. They gather together and set off in groups, headed for warmer climes and a more plentiful supply of food...

Snow geese travel together in groups of several thousand when they migrate.

Many birds die of exhaustion when migrating long distances. Those that cross the Sahara must endure long periods without food.

In Asia, black-headed ibises travel in groups. They fly in a more or less regular fashion, alternating flapping their wings and gliding.

The arctic tern: a bird with stamina

During the northern summer, the arctic tern (*Sterna paradisaea*) settles in the upper latitudes on the edge of the North Pole. Here, the bird nests on coasts which have temporarily lost their thick winter covering of ice and which enjoy long hours of sunlight. The moment the sun begins to disappear, however, at the onset of the six-month-long winter, the tern heads south, all the way to the icy Antarctic, a journey of

The trumpet swan flies with its neck stretched out and its feet tucked up.

more than 18,000 kilometres... Here, the tern can enjoy the brilliance of the southern summer, before returning north to breed. Young terns not yet old enough to breed remain in the Antarctic, waiting until the day when they are old enough to follow the adult birds on the 35,000-kilometre annual round trip.

The swallow: summer's messenger

Every year without fail, during the months of March or April, the swallow returns from its winter absence to grace the skies of the northern hemisphere with its acrobatic flight. Throughout the summer, these tiny birds glide overhead, intermittently swooping to capture the flying insects which are their sole source of nourishment. Thus, when September comes and the shortening days bring cooler weather and the gradual disappearance of insects, the swallow prepares to set off for warmer countries where it will be able to find food. Groups of these forked-tail birds gather on immense perches, such as overhead electricity cables, then set off together to fly south.

The bar-tailed godwit follows coasts and estuaries as it migrates.

As the crane preens itself, it makes its feathers waterproof by covering them with oily secretions from its uropygial gland (situated at the base of its rump).

▼ Swallows are only active during the day (diurnal) and do not travel once night falls. Moving at a speed of around 50 kilometres per hour, those seen in Great Britain in the summer head south across the Mediterranean and the Sahara to reach South Africa and its plentiful supply of insects. During their long migrations, the birds move in stages of approximately 200 kilometres, a distance which is actually less than that covered on a daily basis at home when they are hunting for food.

The wandering albatross: flying close to the waves

From the age of six weeks, the wandering albatross is left in the nest alone.

With a wingspan of around 3.4 metres, the wandering albatross (*Diomedea exulans*) has the longest wings of any bird. They are so long, in fact, that the albatross has considerable difficulty taking off. Once the bird is in the air, however, things improve dramatically. Carried along by the coastal breeze, the albatross allows itself to glide for a few metres, then, once level with the water, it executes a sharp

The extraordinarily long wings of the wandering albatross allow it to glide effortlessly through the air.

The blue-footed booby spends most of its life at sea but comes ashore to breed. Distinctive mating rituals accompany the formation of couples.

turn to face into the wind. This allows the bird to gain height and then descend again towards the waves. Thanks to its perfect mastery of air currents, the albatross can travel for thousands of kilometres without seeming to expend any energy at all, gliding constantly except in the very worst storms. The wandering albatross, which lives in the oceans south of the Tropic of Capricorn, only leaves the open sea to build its nest on the tiny, windswept islands that lie in its path.

As part of mating rituals, wandering albatrosses show off their wingspan.

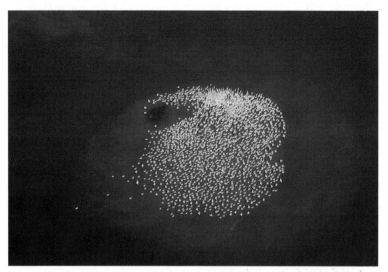

In Kenya, dwarf flamingos sometimes gather together in groups of thousands. These birds live in brackish waters where they are able to find the fish that form their diet.

▼ Migration is common among birds, with almost half of all species making long journeys at specific times of the year. In the majority of cases, the shortening of daylight hours brings on physiological changes such as moulting and the acquisition of extra layers of fat. Thus transformed, the birds are ready to undertake their expedition. During the flight, they usually navigate by means of landmarks such as villages, mountains, rivers and forests. In some species, however, the journey map is inherited genetically.

The white pelican: a giant long-haul bird

The pelican is a fearless creature that will venture into urban areas.

The pelican, a heavyweight in bird terms, is also a long-distance traveller. When flying, it pulls back its neck to support its long beak. During long migratory journeys, pelicans travel together in an arrow-shaped formation. The slipstream created by the bird at the head of the arrow enables the other birds at the back to move more easily through the air. Thus the pelican, which does not glide but has to propel itself purely by wing-power, manages to conserve energy on these exhausting journeys.

The upward flight of the stork

Storks, like cranes or flamingos, sometimes find it difficult to take off, but as soon as they gain some height they fly gracefully and with very little effort. These birds make effective use of warm upward air currents which lift them at a rate of 2 to 3 metres per second. Once they have reached a height of 2,000 to 3,000 metres, storks allow themselves to float until they catch another upward current. Flying in this way, using only the energy required to keep

In order to take off, the pink flamingo has to generate sufficient speed. It runs with its neck stretched out in front, flapping its wings until eventually it leaves the ground.

In Europe, storks used to nest on thatched roofs or in trees. Nowadays, they tend to nest in chimneys or on top of electricity pylons.

As a prelude to migration, cranes gather together as winter approaches.

their long wings spread out, they are able to travel thousands of miles to reach Africa or India, where they spend the winter months.

Travelling in groups

The approach of the migration season brings storks into much closer contact with each other: during this period, the birds gather together in large squadrons which can number several hundred birds.

Male birds of paradise bring a splash of colour to the forests of New Guinea and Indonesia with their bright plumage. The lesser bird of paradise lives on the island of Java.

Tree-dwelling birds

Whether to find food in the form of fruit, pollen or insects, or to build nests, many birds choose to live in trees. With one flap of their wings, they can reach heights inaccessible to other vertebrates and can thus live there in complete safety.

On the island of Guadeloupe in the Caribbean, the Antillean crested hummingbird can hover on the spot and feed without having to land.

I n the trees and undergrowth of the world's forests lies a universe made up entirely of branches and leaves. In order to communicate with each other, most tree-dwelling birds sport vividly coloured plumage or succeed in making themselves heard by characteristic calls...

An all-purpose beak

In the equatorial forests of Africa and Asia, hornbills know how to keep out of sight. When they are not uttering their raucous and

Even the few trees found in deserts attract birds that nest in their branches.

The Blyth's hornbill uses its disproportionately large beak with great precision to shell seeds and catch small animals.

The jay of the forests of Europe feeds principally on acorns. A very timid bird, it flees at the slightest noise, thus sounding the alarm for other animals.

Paradoxically, the multicoloured plumage of the macaw serves as camouflage.

loud call, it is surprisingly difficult to spot these birds in spite of their enormous multicoloured beaks. Endowed with such a useful tool, the largest hornbills feed off fruit, which they peel skilfully, and small animals (insects, snails, frogs), which they knock unconscious and then chop into pieces to make them easier to swallow. When the female is sitting on its eggs, the only contact between male and female is via their beaks. The female sits inside a cavity, such as

The knobbed hornbill has a curved beak with a bony 'helmet' on top.

a hollow tree, and, using her beak, narrows the opening with a mixture of earth and wood, cemented together with her own droppings. Once she has finished, only a small slit remains which the male bird uses to pass food to its mate from the outside.

Birds of paradise

In the semi-darkness of the forests of New Guinea, male birds of paradise spend a great deal of time hiding their brightly

Toucans are noisy inhabitants of the forests of South America. They gather fruit in their beaks and throw it at each other in a playful manner.

The island of Java is home to some extraordinary birds. The king bird of paradise has a bright red back, cobalt blue feet and two long thread-like tail feathers that curl into spirals.

coloured plumage so as not to attract predators. During the mating season, however, they throw such caution to the wind and emerge from their hiding places in the hope of attracting a mate. In the case of the raggiana bird of paradise, male demonstrations of prowess resemble an elaborate beauty contest. The hopeful suitors all gather together on one tree, each trying to occupy the most central branch. The females, meanwhile, secure themselves a ringside seat and wait for the show to begin. Each male then performs a song, and if a female shows any interest in his warblings, the artist follows up this song with a colourful dance. He first raises his wings to form a fan shape which he flaps forwards, then raises his long red tail-feathers to complete the colourful display.

The colour of the hyacinth macaw allows it to blend in to the forest shadows.

An explosion of colours and song

Despite its brightly coloured plumage, the macaw is also an expert in camouflage, able to disappear with ease into the dense vegetation of the tropical forests of America. Busy but discreet, the macaw only rarely makes a public appearance. Thus, when at dawn a group of macaws

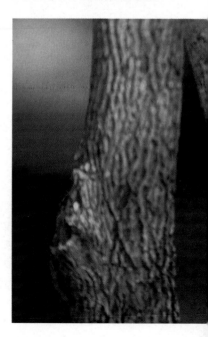

Mynah birds travel through the forests of Asia in search of fruit and insects. In captivity, these birds are able to imitate the sound of the human voice.

▼ Some birds have an amazing capacity to imitate the human voice. The Amazon parrot and the macaw of South America, the grey parrot of Africa, the cockatoo of Australia and the mynah bird of Asia are the most talented of the imitators. Surprisingly, in the wild these birds do not appear to copy the sounds of their environment but only emit loud raucous noises. Away from their natural habitat, however, and placed in contact with human beings, they begin to imitate certain noises. Could it just be their way of killing time?

leave their roots in search of food, there is a sudden explosion of yellow, red, green and blue feathers in the trees. Only once they have all settled down and are eating does calm return to the forest. If disturbed, these birds will show their anger by emitting loud, piercing, harsh cries, but the group will only flee if the threat of danger persists.

Birds in miniature

Hummingbirds are so tiny and so light (just a few centimetres in

In Africa, the roller only leaves its lookout post during the hottest part of the day.

Hummingbirds use up a lot of energy when beating their wings, and are always glad of the opportunity to rest while gathering nectar from a flower.

Hovering delicately, supported only by the force of its tiny wings, the hummingbird plunges its long beak deep into flowers to extract the nectar with its tongue.

length and weighing only a few grams) that some of them can build their nest on a leaf. Once its two minuscule eggs have hatched, the female broad-billed hummingbird (*Cynanthus latirostris*) flies off in search of food. Its flexible wings beat at an extraordinary rate, allowing it to make sharp turns, stop suddenly, and even fly backwards! In the course of its travels, it will suddenly plunge its long beak into a flower, then, once it has reached the corolla, suck out the nectar from inside.

The greater spotted woodpecker picks insect larvae out of the tree bark.

The nightingale (*Luscinia megarhynchos*) sports a brown, cream and rust plumage that acts as an effective camouflage in the thickets where it lives.

▼ Cuckoos do not bother to build a nest. Instead, the females use the nests of other birds, laying their eggs and then abandoning them to the care of the nest's owners. As soon as it is hatched, the young cuckoo sets about getting rid of all competition for food, pushing any other eggs or young out of the nest. At only four days old, the young parasite begins to demand food from its adoptive parents. The red colour on the inside of its beak encourages the adults to feed it faster.

World-class singers

The lark usually occupies a small, well-demarcated territory, to which other birds are not welcome. Nevertheless, it makes its presence felt by spending most of the day and night singing. During the day its song is obscured by that of other birds, but once evening comes only the lark continues, and its beautiful tones can be heard ringing out clearly through the sleeping forest. Almost through-out the night, the lark carries on singing, the pure, clear melody punctuated by harsher, more grating tones.

Blue tits make their nests in small holes that they have found in trees.

Spending the winter together

During the cold season, tits stay in groups for safety. They go everywhere in small bands, and are often joined by other species of climbing birds such as woodpeckers and treecreepers. Sticking together gives these birds a better chance of avoiding danger and of finding food. Throughout the day they call out to each other to keep the group intact and, if danger threatens, each bird is capable of emitting a warning cry which will be understood by all of the other birds in the group.

Birds of prey are characterized by a piercing gaze and hooked beak, exemplified here by the fierce-looking bald eagle.

Hunters by day or night

Birds of prey can be divided into two groups according to when they are active: those that hunt during the day, and those that hunt at night. In a further division, some of those that are active in the daytime hunt live prey, while the others, known as vultures, feed on dead animals.

Nocturnal birds of prey are able to find their way in the dark thanks to their excellent eyesight and their acute sense of hearing.

Birds of prey differ from other birds by two easily distinguishable physical characteristics: a hooked beak and sharp talons. They are carnivorous and use these appendages to tear up prey, which they are able to spot using their extremely sharp eyesight that is sometimes aided by an equally sharp sense of hearing.

The acrobatics of the bald eagle

Although they usually occupy a

The bald-headed vulture eats only the innards and flesh of dead animals.

The bald eagle only eats fish. It chooses a suitable vantage point near the water, then swoops down to catch its prey when the latter comes near the surface.

The goshawk is an excellent hunter. As soon as it spots its prey, it swoops down on it with such speed and precision that there is no chance of escape.

specific individual territory, during the winter months bald eagles (*Haliaeetus leucocephalus*) group together. This enables them to increase the efficiency of their search for food, and also gives young birds an opportunity to find a mate. During this period, the bald eagle, usually extremely aggressive towards its fellows, exhibits a radical change in behaviour. Groups of birds perform dizzying feats of aerial acrobatics which look for all the world like games. For example,

The little owl nests in dark and sheltered places, such as this hollow tree trunk.

The gyrfalcon hunts by swooping low over the ground. Its favourite prey are rabbits and other small rodents, but it will also eat other birds.

The steppe eagle can often be found with vultures around an animal carcass.

one bird will grab a small branch in its talons, fly up high, and then drop it. The bird's companions then launch themselves towards the branch, in an effort to 'capture' it before it reaches the ground.

The golden eagle defines its territory

The adult life of a golden eagle begins with the search for a territory. In order to feed itself, the eagle concentrates on one particular area of its domain, to

The African fish-eagle is highly skilled at fishing on the wing. It has even been known to attack pelicans to steal their catch of fish.

Among eagles, it is often the male that is responsible for building the nest.

which outsiders are aggressively denied entry. Only the eagle's mate, with whom he is often united for life, has the right to enter the hunting zone. Directed by the female, the couple builds several eyries (nests), spread out over the whole domain. The female chooses the nest in which she wishes to lay her eggs, while the other eyries are used as resting places during hunting expeditions or during the night, or even as a place in which to store surplus food that has been collected.

The buzzard, a common European bird, has a very varied diet, ranging from worms or snails to small rabbits.

Weighing on average only around 4 kilos, the Verreaux's eagle thinks nothing of attacking a baboon. It will even try to steal the remains of a leopard's kill.

The peregrine falcon: an expert hunter

Although small in stature, the peregrine falcon is a giant when it comes to flight. No other bird, even among birds of prey, is able to rival this bird as it folds in its wings and aims for the ground at a record speed of 360 kilometres per hour. Using this skill to full advantage, the peregrine falcon feeds exclusively on small birds, which it captures mid-flight. One of its methods of attack consists of diving on its prey and, at the

The osprey captures fish while they are still swimming underwater.

moment when it is about to pass, striking it violently with its talons. The victim does not always give in on this first attack but is usually sufficiently weakened by it to succumb on the second. The falcon will finish it off with a blow to the neck with its beak, then take it somewhere quiet to tear it to pieces.

The lazy life of the Andean condor

The favourite pastime of the Andean condor (*Vultur gryphus*), like that of many other birds of prey, is the arduous task of taking a siesta. More than fifteen hours of every day are dedicated to this activity, perched on a rocky ledge, and only hunger can coax the bird from its lethargy. When that happens, the condor leaves its resting place and goes to join its fellows in the search for an appetizing meal. Thanks to a wingspan of more than 3 metres, condors are able to glide effortlessly on the powerful upward air currents that pass through the mountain regions of its natural habitat. Once one condor spots a dead animal on the ground, it begins its descent. The others swiftly follow, anxious not to miss the feast and keen to plunge their long featherless

The king vulture lives in the tropical forests of South America.

The lappet-faced vulture lands in the middle of a group of white-backed African griffon vultures, too busy picking at the carcass to notice the new arrival.

▼ Some Egyptian vultures add eggs to their diet of dead animals. To eat a small egg such as that of a pelican, the vulture simply takes the egg in its beak and breaks it by dropping it on a rock. A larger egg, such as that of an ostrich, however, calls for a slightly more sophisticated technique. The vulture chooses a stone, takes it in its beak, positions itself above the egg, then drops the stone. It repeats this operation until it succeeds in smashing the egg open.

The barn owl is covered in feathers from head to toe. This effectively muffles the bird's movements, allowing it to hunt in almost total silence.

necks deep into the corpse. The only sign of the condors' presence will be a gleaming white skeleton, picked clean of every last trace of flesh. After this banquet, each bird returns to its perch for a feather-cleaning session, an essential routine, before setting off again over the valleys of the Andes.

The sharp senses of the barn owl

A night bird, the barn owl (*Tyto alba*) emerges only at dusk,

A long-eared owl keeps watch in the dead of night.

The eagle owl prefers to hunt at dawn or dusk. It eats small animals whole, then later regurgitates the bones and fur in the form of a ball.

The young great grey owls are kept sufficiently warm by a layer of down that their mother does not have to sit on them.

▼ Nocturnal birds of prey have two major advantages when it comes to night vision: their eyeballs are elongated, throwing a magnified image on to the retina; and the retina itself is capable of registering even the slightest glimmer of light. An owl's eyes are limited in their movement and are placed side by side on the front of the bird's face, so the owl can only see what is directly in front of it. However, owls are able to rotate their heads by almost 360 degrees, so nothing escapes their piercing gaze.

The snowy owl's white plumage blends in with the snow-covered tundra.

when there is no longer any risk of meeting its arch-enemy, the crow. Thanks to its excellent night vision, the barn owl is able to hunt even in the last glimmers of daylight. Slowly and silently, the owl surveys its territory. It has a flat heart-shaped face designed so that even the slightest sound reaches its ears. Thus, when night falls, the owl compensates for the loss of visibility with its acute sense of hearing.

The hunting techniques of the great grey owl

The great grey owl inhabits the northern regions of Europe, Asia and North America, where it has to survive in an environment that varies radically according to the seasons. It must therefore adapt its hunting methods to climatic changes and to the quantity of food available. If the owl needs to feed its young, it flies backwards and forwards along its territory in search of small rodents. When the bird is alone, on the other hand, it contents itself with lying in wait for passing prey. In the winter, the owl has to rely on its sense of hearing to detect the movements of its prey, even when the latter is hidden beneath snow.

The down of a young king penguin is brown and very thick. This 'fleece' protects the young bird against the freezing cold of the Antarctic winter.

Flightless birds

Although the ability to fly developed early on in the evolution of birds, several species, such as the ostrich, the turkey and the penguin, to name but a few, are, to this day, unable to fly. Confined to the ground, these birds have each developed their own particular way of overcoming their flightlessness.

Although the ostrich boasts feathers aplenty, it is still incapable of flight. By way of compensation, however, it can run as fast as a galloping horse.

Although not every bird can fly, all birds can use their two feet to walk. The ratite family, which includes the ostrich, the emu, the cassowary and the kiwi, are all excellent runners. It is likely that their ancestors were better at flying but, over the centuries, these birds have become bigger and bigger and their ability to fly has decreased in direct proportion to their increased bulk. Other birds, such as the penguin or the auk, have lost the ability to fly but have acquired that of swimming

The wings of the lesser rhea are incapable of lifting it off the ground.

King penguins move over the icy wastes of the islands bordering the Antarctic Circle by waddling proudly along on their strong broad feet.

The ostrich has two large wings whose only purpose is to impress prospective partners during the mating season.

underwater. In the case of penguins, their inability to defy gravity is explained by an increase in their body density, which enables them to swim better but does them no favours where flight is concerned!

The ostrich: a giant bird of the desert

The ostrich has the proud distinction of holding a number of records in the bird world. With a height that can reach up to 2.75 metres, and a weight of nearly 150 kilograms in the male, it is

The peacock, despite its abundant plumage, is a poor flier.

The southern cassowary paces the forests of Australia and New Guinea. It is not a good idea to get in the way of this 80-kilo bird when it is running at full speed!

the largest bird on the planet. It also has the longest neck. In evolving as a runner, the ostrich, a native of Africa, has reduced the number of digits on its feet: it is the only bird to possess only two toes rather than the more usual three. This physical peculiarity enables the ostrich to reach speeds of around 70 kilometres per hour and to leap over objects up to 1.5 metres high. It may not be able to fly, but an ostrich that is being pursued by a predator can keep

The emu looks down on the world from a height of 1.8 metres.

up an average speed of 40 kilometres per hour for as long as half an hour.

The ratite family

The ostrich does not have a monopoly on a large body, long legs and a long neck. Other members of the ratite family (the group of flightless running birds) share similar traits. The closest, physically speaking, is the emu. A native of Australia, the main features that distinguish this bird from its African cousin are the

In contrast to the ostrich, the rhea has feathers on its neck.

The plump 'thighs' of the ostrich correspond to human calves. When they run, ostriches grip the ground with their toes.

fact that it has three toes, not two, and that its neck and upper legs are covered with feathers. The rhea, which inhabits the pampas plains of South America, looks like a small ostrich with no long tail feathers. The Australian cassowaries are the brightest of the group, with a multicoloured head and bony crest. The purpose of the crest is to protect the bird's head when it makes its way through the dense forests where it lives. With its short legs and long slender beak, the tiny kiwi is perhaps the most unusual member of the ratite family. It leads a quiet hidden existence in the forests of New Zealand, even going as far as laying its eggs in a hole in the ground!

Unlike other members of the ratite family, the kiwi is nocturnal.

Birds that prefer climbing to flying

Although capable of flight, many birds, such as the peacock, the pheasant, the turkey and other farmyard fowl, spend most of the daytime on the ground. At night, the peacock takes refuge in a tree to sleep, joining the other members of its family. Ill-equipped for flying, it takes a great deal of effort for this bird just to make the short journey as far as the bottom branches. It continues up to the top of the tree

Ostrich young are well camouflaged and hard to spot in the savannah. Their feathers are striped on the neck and speckled on the body.

▼ Turkeys, guinea fowl, quails, cocks and chickens are all reared by humans for their flesh and, in some cases, for their eggs. This domestication, which has gone on for more than five thousand years, has been accompanied by a form of artificial selection. Humans have always tried to obtain the fattest possible specimens of these birds, as they provide the most meat. Thus, poor fliers to start with, certain species of birds have become completely incapable of flight.

by climbing from branch to branch. Coming down, on the other hand, is a far simpler affair: the peacock just spreads its wings and jumps. Although its feathers may not be much use for flying, the male possesses a set of tail feathers that make it a guaranteed success with the females of the species. With its tail fanned out to display a magnificent array of shimmering colours, a young and healthy peacock is capable of seducing up to five female birds (peahens) in succession.

The markings of the king penguin are brighter during the mating season.

To protect themselves against the freezing wind, emperor penguins huddle in a kind of rotating scrum. Each bird takes it in turn to bear the brunt of the wind on its back.

Emperor penguins live in colonies with their young on the pack ice of the Antarctic. The young are grouped together in 'crèches' from the age of around one and a half months.

Diving birds

The emperor penguin inhabits one of the most inhospitable regions of the globe: the Antarctic. Its thick and completely waterproof covering of feathers and thick layer of body fat provide the bird with sufficient insulation to withstand temperatures as low as −50ºC. Although completely unable to fly and distinctly ungainly on land, the penguin is an excellent swimmer, leaping into the freezing Antarctic waters in pursuit of food.

Adelie penguins dive off the icy cliffs into the sea to hunt for food.

Little penguins nest in the open. As soon as the young are able to fly, they head swiftly for the ocean to escape from predators on land.

▼ Depending where it is and what it is doing, the puffin uses its webbed feet in different ways. When flying, it tucks them up behind to compensate for the limited lift afforded by its short neck. To stop, it simply brings them forward. On the surface of the water, the puffin swims by paddling, whilst underwater it uses its feet only as a rudder. On land, its feet, which are set far back on its body, give the puffin an awkward gait and it is forced to waddle...just like the common duck.

Taking to swimming...like a duck to water

In this aquatic environment, the small stiff wings of the emperor penguin are used not to fly, but also to propel its streamlined body through the water at speeds of up to 30 kilometres per hour. Like a torpedo, the bird pursues the fish and crustaceans that abound in these waters, using its webbed feet as a rudder. So streamlined is its body that, when the penguin moves on to the pack ice to lay its eggs, it takes advantage of even the slightest slope in the ice to slide itself into the water rather than walking! Swimming and flying require totally different physical qualities – body density or a broad wingspan – but the rhea and the guillemots, which also spend a large amount of time near water, have at least preserved the ability to launch themselves into the air even though the narrow span of their wings means that they have to work very hard to get from the shore to the open sea. However, once under the water, they move with remarkable ease and grace, swimming along by flapping their wings up and down in a strange action that looks very much like underwater flying.

The rockhopper climbs over rocks with the aid of sharp claws.

Birds in
OUR
WORLD

Falconry requires some simple but indispensable equipment: a padded leather glove for the bird to perch on and a hood to keep its head in darkness.

Called into service

While many of us dream of being 'as free as a bird', our feathered friends have long been exploited by man. All over the world, birds are used for such varied tasks as hunting, fishing, carrying messages and fertilizing crops.

The inhabitants of the Greek island of Tinos were inspired by traditional architectural forms when they built their dovecotes.

B efore humans learned the art of animal husbandry, hunting was their only means of procuring meat. As early man ventured out in his quest for food he would, in those areas to which the birds were native, have enjoyed watching the impressive raptors hunting their prey. Imagine the mixture of admiration and jealousy that those primitive humans must have felt in the face of these superb shows of power and precision. Naturally enough, they soon developed ways of using the birds for their own ends.

A cockerel, a chicken and their fluffy chicks in a 15th-century Chinese painting.

Dovecotes are home to carrier pigeons as well as doves. Among other species, non-working birds are raised either for their beautiful appearance or for their meat.

In the North African souks, locals proudly show off their falcons to passers-by. Beneath their hoods, the birds remain oblivious to the crowds.

The early falconers

The first attempts to domesticate birds of prey and train them to hunt for man were made long ago; the earliest evidence we have unearthed dates back about 3500 years. In Mesopotamia, sculptures have been found that depict ancient hawking scenes, clearly showing men holding falcons on a leash. The Egyptian, Greek and Roman civilizations seem to have neglected falconry but ancient writings describe its practice in Asia. The Greek

Ostrich feathers were once highly prized by the clothing industry.

A peregrine enjoys a novel vantage point from which to observe its surroundings!

historian Ctesias tells us of hunters in northern India enlisting the aid of eagles. Gradually, falconry then spread across the Far East, as far as Japan.

A passion strong enough to unite the bitterest foes

Europeans had their first taste of falconry at the time of the Germanic invasions, towards the end of the fourth century, but the sport did not really catch on until the Middle Ages. Medieval lords, the only stratum of

In daylight, nocturnal birds of prey may be attacked by other species. Cunning huntsmen know this and use the raptors as bait for their intended prey.

The larger birds of prey are rarely used in hawking. Majestic birds such as this one, however, are in great demand at historical pageants.

The falcon's hood must be exactly the right size for the bird's head. The bird must be able to move its neck freely and open its beak.

society allowed to own a bird of prey, learned a great deal from the Moors who settled in Spain during the course of the eighth century. The Moors in their turn owed much to the Arabs and Persians, who for centuries had been carefully recording their ideas about the training and care of these fierce but beautiful birds in manuals of falconry. The crusades provided another learning opportunity. The European nobles taught their Middle Eastern opponents how to use dogs to flush out the prey and

Back in the 13th-century, Gengis Khan enjoyed the sport of falconry.

to help the falcon make a kill. In exchange, they returned to their lands with two indispensable tools: the lure (made of feathers and meat), which coaxes the falcon home with its catch; and the hood, which covers the bird's eyes and keeps it calm and still.

A deep-rooted Arab tradition

It was in the Middle East that the history of falconry really began and it is here, appropriately enough, that the sport continues to

In Tunisia, sparrowhawks train for a long period before being used in hunting.

14th-century falconry texts recommend that handlers spray their bird's chest with water to calm it. In Kuwait, this technique is still used to quench the bird's thirst.

be most keenly pursued. To this day, the Gulf princes regularly organize sumptuous hunting parties which have been known to last up to a month. Under the desert skies, rank is forgotten and hosts and guests alike become oblivious to all but the falcon's hunting prowess. In the evening, talk around the fire turns inevitably to the day's exploits.

Hunting birds and fighter planes

In the West, the vogue for hawking went into decline from the 17th century onwards. Nowadays, the few raptors that are used for hunting are mostly bred in captivity. Apart from hunting, these birds are also put to slightly more unusual uses. For many years now, airport runways have been the workplace of both birds of prey and those somewhat larger metal birds we call planes. It is the job of specially trained falcons and goshawks to patrol the area and scare off the birds that choose to nest at the side of the runways, often in large numbers. Partridges, lapwings and crows all have a habit of wandering across the runway in search of food whenever the fancy takes them. If an aircraft were to hit the runway at the same

As soon as the planes have left the runway, the goshawks are released.

The air force relies on goshawks to keep the skies above the airfield clear of intruders. Talented fliers, these birds sometimes seem to outdo even the planes themselves.

▼ In parts of China and Japan, cormorants help fishermen in their work. The small fishing boats head for the open sea or along rivers to the fishing grounds, where the fishermen tie a cord around their cormorants' necks and then release them into the water to dive for fish. Before long, the birds resurface with the prey in their gullets, the cord preventing them from swallowing the fish completely. The fishermen haul the cormorants back in and, pressing down hard on the back of the birds' necks, make them relinquish their catch.

time, the birds would stand every chance of being sucked into one of its engines...doing some serious damage to both the plane and the bird itself!

The pigeon: a discreet and reliable messenger

The carrier pigeon has long been prized for its unerring navigational skills. Released hundreds of miles from home, the bird instantly sets off on its return course. Since ancient times, writers including Aristotle and

Dovecotes were often built to reflect the power of their privileged owners.

As late as World War 1, carrier pigeons were a vital part of the communication network between regiments. Some birds were even presented with military honours after a battle.

Carrier pigeons take messages back to their roosts, in the form of a note attached to one of their feet.

The pigeon's glamorous cousin, the turtle-dove, is very popular with bird-fanciers.

Pliny the Elder have described how people have bred pigeons for express use as messengers. When the Roman armies went on campaign, they were sure to take a supply of carrier pigeons with them, sending back news of the legions' progress to Rome by attaching messages to the birds' necks. Back at its roost, the carrier pigeon would surrender the missive with which it had been entrusted. By setting up a string of roosting places at regular intervals all over the countryside,

The largest pigeon in Europe, the wood pigeon has never been domesticated. It has, however, adapted extremely well to the unnatural environment created by our cities.

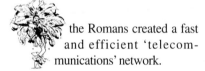

the Romans created a fast and efficient 'telecommunications' network.

Pigeon-fancying takes off

With the advent of the telephone and broadcasting, professional carrier pigeons were able to retire and devote themselves to more leisurely pursuits. In the early 19th century, pigeon-fancying was popular with working people in much of northern Europe. The birds' owners were constantly on the lookout for a champion who

At the end of a race, the arrival time of each bird must be recorded.

The architectural style and composition of dovecotes echo the human dwellings of a particular region. In Egypt, these buildings are designed to protect birds from the heat.

Barely two days old, these tiny turkeys are crowded together in vast cages. Depending on farming methods, the birds will either stay locked up or be allowed into the fields.

Cockerels and chickens enjoy gardens where they are sure to find worms.

could take part in competitions over distances ranging from 50 kilometres to 1000 kilometres.

From the farmyard to the cooking pot

A familiar sight the world over, the farmyard chicken can trace its history back more than 5000 years to India and to a jungle fowl belonging to the *Gallus* genus. Valued for both its meat and its eggs, easy to feed and relatively simple to look after, the domestic chicken soon became a success story all around the world. At the same time, other birds were also being bred for food: the duck, goose, turkey, pigeon and latterly even the ostrich. The first farm to specialize in ostriches was set up in 1838 in South Africa; since then, ostrich farming has spread to North Africa, the United States and Europe. Originally bred for its feathers, the ostrich is now farmed for its eggs, its meat and the leather that can be obtained from its skin.

To make foie gras, ducks and geese are fattened up by force-feeding.

Of all the members of the bird kingdom, the ostrich lays the biggest and strongest eggs. Each egg can weigh up to 1.35 kilos.

The macaw family boasts some of the most magnificent plumage of all; the colours include a splendid combination of red, yellow, blue and green.

In Peru, guano is still an important source of income. Conditions are very harsh for the workers, however, who have to carry it up the side of cliffs.

In Malaysia, specialized shops sell birds' nests for making into soup.

Some other bird products

A speciality of southeast Asia, bird's nest soup is made from the nest of the salangane (a species of swift). Unlike its more common cousin who uses mud in the construction of its nest, the salangane uses its saliva to bind the building materials together. The outer part of the nest is used to make the well-known spicy soup. On another continent, mid-19th-century Peru experienced a spell of prosperity thanks to its

The eider is a large duck which nests in the far north. The hunting of eider is strictly forbidden so the feathers have to be collected after the female has moulted.

▼ Towards the end of the 19th century, no self-respecting lady of fashion would have been seen without a clutch of bright feathers to complete her outfit. Plumes from the ostrich, the bird of paradise, the parrot or the peacock became finishing touches for a hairstyle, were transformed into a fan or were draped round the shoulders in the form of an elegant feather boa. Wild birds were relentlessly pursued and killed for their feathers without thought for the future survival of the species.

The eider's cosy nest is lined with down to keep in the heat.

huge reserves of bird droppings, or 'guano'. Very rich in nitrate, guano was exported and sold to farmers as a fertilizer.

The writer's quill

The invention of the quill pen marked an important step forward in the history of writing materials. In use since the sixth century, the quill offered an accuracy and ease of use that the brush and reed did not afford. A crow's feather was deemed to be the best choice for fine strokes, whereas a goose's or swan's feather was considered most suitable for everyday use. Whatever the purpose or source, the feather was always taken from the bird's wingtip.

From quills to quilts

Thanks to its ability to trap pockets of air between the soft fine feathers, down provides superlative heat retention. What is more, it has a very low mass in relation to its volume. These two factors make down an ideal choice in the manufacture of anoraks and eiderdowns. Depending on which part of the world you live in, down may come from the eider duck, the goose, the swan or even the albatross.

Tiny house sparrows are far from shy. They quickly get used to being around people, especially if they are offered food.

Observation and conservation

The relationship between birds and humans is not always without complications. Not content with simply watching and admiring, people are often quick to harm birds. If we are to continue to enjoy sharing the world with our feathered friends, we must start to take better care of them.

Black-headed gulls use the precision of their flight to delight their spectators by catching pieces of bread in mid-air.

P eople are not just interested in birds because of their usefulness or the profit to be made from them. We also value them for their often splendid feathers, their harmonious song and the elegance of their flight.

Birds as pets

Endlessly fascinated by the members of the bird kingdom, some people wish to be surrounded by them all day, every day, and have no qualms

A seagull surveys the scene from a convenient perch.

Identifying birds in the wild requires a great deal of patience, the right equipment (a pair of binoculars or a telescope) and a reputable field guide.

Pigeons have made their home in Paris for more than 200 years and are today as much a part of the cityscape as many of the city's best known monuments.

Fluttering around its cage, this small bird fills a home with its song.

about removing them from their natural habitat in order to keep them in cages and aviaries. Quite how long ago people first started keeping birds in captivity is not known. It is, for example, difficult to say just when the infatuation of the South American Indians with the parrots of the Amazon basin began. On the other hand, we do know that in the fourth century BC, Onesicritus, captain of Alexander the Great's fleet, returned from an expedition to

the banks of the Indus with strange booty: several live parakeets. This species, christened Alexander's parakeet but later known as the African grey parrot, was popular with the Greeks and Romans. Even at this early date, their owners were charmed by their ability to mimic human speech. Pliny the Elder, in his wisdom, advised hitting uncooperative birds over the head with 'a stick as hard as a parrot's beak' to speed up the learning process!

Though a protected species, macaws sometimes fall prey to smugglers.

The canary, the budgerigar and the turtledove, long bred in captivity, have adapted well to life behind bars.

The cockatoo can be recognized by the large and usually brightly coloured crest on top of its head. Its name comes from the Malay word 'kakatua', which means 'pincers'.

Caged birds

In the late 15th century, the golden age of voyages of exploration and the discoveries of hitherto unknown lands, Europeans started to bring back brightly coloured birds from their travels. Their expeditions provided a steady supply of specimens for the market stalls at home, and the birdcages of the West gradually filled up with a whole range of exotic species. The trade in tropical birds continues to this day, often causing them great suffering. Nowadays, however, bird-lovers are just as likely to be interested in the home-grown variety found in their own backyards.

In winter, birds are easy to watch as they often come close to our homes.

Purpose-built accommodation

The spread of our towns and cities has brought in its wake a decrease in possible nesting sites. Every hedge that is ripped out, every dead tree that is chopped down and every old wall that is demolished means one less home for the local bird population. It is an easy task, however, to replace these natural sites with nesting boxes. The dimensions of the miniature bird huts must be carefully matched to the size and behavioural characteristics of the

The collared dove enjoys the company of people. Never straying far from its territory, it likes to make its nest in the parks and gardens of our towns and villages.

In temperate climates, birds need to be able to survive the cold season. To fight against low temperatures, they must have a nutritious diet, yet at that time of year such food is increasingly scarce. This is where we can all help by ensuring a rich and varied food supply for them to eat. A healthy diet would consist of animal or vegetable fats, grains (rice or sunflower seeds, for example), nuts, apples and water. In the absence of a special bird-feeder, simply lay the items on a branch or hang them in a mesh bag from it.

species you wish to attract. For example, the opening must be small enough to protect the nestlings from the wind and the cold but big enough, of course, for the parent birds to squeeze through. For tits, a diameter of less than 3 centimetres is about right; for starlings, it should be around 4.5 centimetres; and for little owls, 7 centimetres. The nesting box should be hung from a branch, ideally between 2 and 6 metres from the ground, and the entrance hole sheltered from prevailing winds.

Hides are the best places for ornithologists to observe migrating birds.

The carrier pigeon is the only bird to have been used for delivering messages, but that hasn't stopped the owners of this mailbox from decorating it with pictures of other birds.

No need for trick photography to get this shot of a peregrine in front of the Empire State Building in New York. These raptors sometimes nest on top of skyscrapers.

Birdwatching

For a long time, people only studied those birds that were of use to man. Treatises on hunting from the ancient world and the Middle Ages are packed with advice for rearing and looking after those birds of prey destined for a career hunting on man's behalf. Then, with the development of the natural sciences and the growth in the number of scientific expeditions taking place in the late 18th and the 19th centuries, notably those led by the English naturalist Charles Darwin and the French

Weighing a young albatross is all part of an ornithologist's work.

A car speeding along straight Australian roads can spell death for an unsuspecting bird that is busy with something else and slow to recognize the approaching danger.

explorer Jules Dumont d'Urville, interest spread to all species and became a scientific discipline in its own right: ornithology. Amateurs, too, were more than willing to use their leisure time to pursue their passion; it was they who put together the first field guides.

Mankind's victims

In spite of the vigilance of bird-lovers the world over, the activities of the human race constantly put entire bird populations at risk. Hunting, the most obvious danger,

Every year, many birds are electrocuted by power cables.

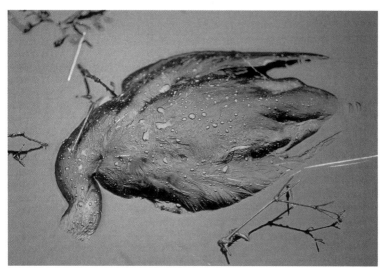

According to statistics, cormorants are among the worst affected by oil slicks, but other birds, such as this poor mallard, also perish after contact with oil.

Unscrupulous smugglers are known to hunt South American parrots. The birds are killed and their feathers sold.

Many bird species have already become extinct and the number is destined to increase even further as a result of our shortsightedness. We can only mourn the passing of the dodo, which was still alive in Mauritius as late as the 17th century. The size of a turkey, this flightless bird was killed off by European settlers and their domestic animals, such as cats and pigs, greedy for eggs and chicks. The American passenger pigeon, similarly, has been hunted to the brink of extinction — now not a single bird of this species survives in the wild.

Seagulls sometimes meet their end in the search for food.

may threaten whole species when it is practised on too large a scale. Killing parrots in the Amazon basin and shooting birds on their migratory routes, for example, have an immediate and drastic effect on numbers. Less visible but even more dangerous, the pesticides and insecticides used by farmers poison many insect-eating birds. And last but not least, many sea birds also fall victim to oil slicks.

Coming to the aid of endangered species

Forced to acknowledge the dangers facing many bird species, we are finally starting to put some long-overdue emergency measures in place. In the Netherlands, for example, the state gives farmers compensation for the crops eaten by swans that spend winter on their land. In the Alps, lammergeiers raised in captivity have been released in areas where the species is threatened. In California, the condor has been saved from extinction thanks to stringent conservation measures including the breeding of these birds in captivity. Yet many other species, including the kagu of New Caledonia, still need our help if their continued survival is to be ensured.

In this work by Bartholomäus Zeitblom (1497, Bucharest Art Gallery), a dove is used to symbolize the Holy Spirit visiting Mary.

Birds in mythology

Born of an egg and capable of soaring up to the heavens, birds have always been seen to possess godlike qualities... Hawk, ibis, eagle, swan and dove have all taken their place in the pantheon of the gods, but when men try to emulate their feathered idols in flight, they fall, Icarus-like, from grace.

On Egyptian papyri, the hawk-headed god of the Sun, Horus, is often depicted bearing the pharaoh's headdress.

A s the only creatures able to move around the earth on the surface of the sea and in the sky, birds, from the gentle dove to the powerful eagle, have always captured our imagination. From the earliest times, they have been central to our myths and legends in which they symbolize a range of qualities.

The ibis: an Egyptian deity

The ibis figured significantly in the Egyptian pantheon, where it was known by the name of Thoth. God of the Moon, Thoth was

An Australian petroglyph, believed to be 15,000 years old, showing an emu.

Fra Angelico depicts the angel Gabriel with multicoloured wings, announcing to Mary that she is to be the Mother of Christ (fresco, c. 1440, Convent of San Marco, Florence).

Horus, with his hawk's head and a plumed headdress, adorns the wall of an Egyptian tomb in Thebes.

protector of the arts, inventions and magic. He created hieroglyphs, which enabled him to record the other gods' decisions, and he even appointed himself their spokesperson. As a record-keeper and an inventor, he was worshiped by both scribes and magicians.

Horus: the hawk god

In the tales of Egyptian mythology, Horus is presented as one of several different gods. Most often he is depicted as the hawk-headed god of the sky with his piercing

Thoth watches over the temple of Ramses II at Abydos in Egypt.

In Edfu, an imposing statue of Horus guards the entrance to his temple.

eyes shown as the Sun and the Moon. Horus was the son of the goddess Isis and the god Osiris. Osiris, the King of Egypt, was bitterly envied by his brother Seth, the god of violence and storms. Seth killed Osiris and, when he grew up, Horus in turn killed Seth to avenge his father's death and reclaim the throne of Egypt. It is said that the goddess Isis laid a trap for Seth in order to help her son. Having changed into a pretty woman, she went to meet Seth, pretending to be a shepherd's widow. She explained that her

Deified by the ancient Egyptians as the god Thoth, half-human half-bird, the ibis was also represented in Egyptian art in its bird form.

Egyptian symbolism draws heavily on animals. Here, in the temple of Abydos, the god Horus is seen with a cobra and a bull.

son's flock had just been stolen and Seth declared that it was wrong to steal a child's inheritance. Isis changed into a bird and, flying off, proclaimed that Seth had just confessed his own crime: usurping the throne of Egypt and depriving Horus of his rights. To settle the matter, the guilty Seth challenged Horus to a duel, which was won by the rightful heir.

Stormy love affairs in ancient Greece

As well as being the supreme god of Greek mythology, Zeus was also known for his countless amorous exploits. When he turned his attentions to a mere mortal, he was forced to change his form; otherwise the sight of him would bring certain death. Zeus often took on the appearance of an animal, a talent which also frequently enabled him to give his jealous wife, Hera, the slip. When Zeus took a fancy to the youth Ganymede, therefore, he chose to become an eagle, in order to abduct him from his father Tros, King of Troy. As compensation, he offered the king a stable of horses, described as being 'as swift as the storm'. Back on Olympus, Zeus honoured his young protégé by making him cup-bearer to the gods.

Rubens painted Zeus as an eagle come to carry off Ganymede.

Hercules is shown killing the eagle of Zeus which has come to eat the liver of Prometheus as punishment for stealing fire from the gods (bronze Etruscan coffin, 5th century BC).

▼ Artists have often taken myths and legends as their subject matter. Here, the presence of a swan by Zeus' side alludes to the time when the god took the form of a swan to visit Leda, the wife of the King of Sparta. Following their union, Leda gave birth to four children, encased in two eggs. From the first egg emerged Pollux and Helen, from the second Castor and Clytemnestra. Castor and Pollux went off in search of the Golden Fleece; Helen was the cause of the Trojan war; and Clytemnestra murdered her husband, Agamemnon.

Daedalus and the Minotaur

In Greek mythology, Daedalus is renowned for his brilliance. A citizen of Athens, he excelled in architecture, sculpture and mechanics. After killing his nephew Talos, Daedalus was forced to seek refuge with King Minos in Crete. He designed and built the labyrinth to contain the Minotaur, half bull, half-man, who lived on the flesh of young Athenians. Ariadne, the daughter of Minos, undertook to rid the island of the monster with the help of Theseus, son of the King

Fleeing from the labyrinth, Daedalus helps his son Icarus to take off.

Having flown too close to the sun, Icarus loses his wings and falls towards the sea as his father looks on powerless. *Fall of Icarus*, oil painting by Carlo Saraceni, 1607.

The swan, symbol of Lohengrin, the knight of Wagner's opera of the same name, is everywhere at Neuschwanstein. The castle was built by Lugwig II of Bavaria, Wagner's patron.

The Chinese phoenix is linked with the invention of music and dance.

of Athens. She went to Daedalus to ask him how her champion should find his way back out of the labyrinth. Daedalus told her that all Theseus would need was a thread to mark the route he had taken into the maze.

The flight from the labyrinth with Icarus

For giving this advice to Ariadne and thus conspiring in the Minotaur's death, Daedalus was charged with treason. Minos

The 16th-century Italian painter Paolo Veronese here depicts the Holy Spirit as a dove, spreading its wings between the arms of God.

▼ The indigenous peoples of North America revere their totem poles and ritual masks which symbolize Wakan Tanka, the Supreme Being, at the time of the Creation. On earth, his power is represented by the Thunderbird. This gigantic creature often takes the form of an eagle, with flashes of lightning radiating from its beak and eyes. When it flies, the beating of its wings is said to be so powerful that it produces thunderclaps and the bird is said to be so strong that it can even lift a whale into the air.

imprisoned the inventor in his own labyrinth with his son Icarus, but not before the ingenious Daedalus had laid his hands on some feathers and wax. By sticking the feathers on to their arms, father and son were able to escape from their prison by flying. However, young Icarus, dazzled by the sun and intoxicated with his powers of flight, headed straight for the burning star. Ignoring his father's warnings, Icarus flew too close and the wax holding his wings together began to melt. The young man plummeted into the sea, never to resurface.

A baroque image of the Flood on a Mexican church in Tecamachalco.

The dove and Noah's Ark

In the Bible, the Book of Genesis tells us how the world was created; on the fifth day God made the fowl of the air. Later on, bitterly disappointed by the violent behaviour displayed by mankind, he decided to rid the earth of all living things, with the exception of a pair of animals from each species and of one man, Noah, and his family. God ordered Noah to build an ark to shelter the animals and then unleashed the Flood. When the waters had subsided a little, Noah released a dove, which flew off to seek solid ground. In no time at all, the bird returned with an olive branch in its beak.

On this 19th-century German postcard, a young woman deep in discussion with a stork evokes the bird's links with fertility.

Birds as symbols

From the heraldic eagle, a universal symbol of power, to the baby-bringing stork of northern Europe, many different powers and virtues have at some point been attributed to birds. Even today, we continue to see these feathered creatures all around us in art, literature and advertising.

The product of a fighter pilot's imagination, Jonathan Livingston Seagull is a young bird in love with liberty, whose only preoccupation is flying for pleasure.

For humans, birds have come to symbolize many things. Different cultures focus on particular species that embody the values they seek to promote in their society.

From the Roman eagle to the Gallic cockerel

In ancient Rome, the eagle was used as a symbol by the militia and found its way on to the insignia of the legions. This large bird of prey, with its sharp talons and hooked beak, embodies the

The two-headed eagle is a common symbol of power in Eastern Europe.

Adopted as the symbol of the United States in 1782, the bald eagle embodies the ideals of a nation that wishes to be united, brave, strong and generous.

Hens' eggs used to be a traditional Easter dish. Throughout Europe, chocolate eggs are still given as gifts. In Germany, they are said to be delivered by hares.

Inspired by the Bible, the dove is the international symbol of peace.

desire for conquest and glory that typified the Roman Empire. Later, the bird reappeared on the coat of arms of the Germanic emperors, then on the colours of all those who dreamed of inheriting Rome's power; the eagle has become the emblem of many powerful Western empires. When Napoleon Bonaparte came to power in France, uniforms, monuments and flags all gained an eagle, which even replaced the Gallic cockerel. Symbol of the French nation, the latter can trace

its origins back to a pun on the Latin word *gallus*, which means both 'Gaul' and 'cockerel'.

The cockerel has been the symbol of France since the time of the Gauls.

Feathers and traditional finery

In societies all over the world, feathers have long been used to decorate ceremonial costumes. For Native Americans, such as the Iroquois or the Sioux, the golden eagle is a symbol of virility and a mark of the warrior. Tradition used to demand that every youth

In Papua New Guinea, men attend religious festivals wearing headdresses decorated with a stunning array of exotic feathers.

Native Americans work feathers from the eagle and the turkey into their striking ceremonial headdresses.

on the brink of manhood hunt down an eagle for its feathers. In a completely different culture, the Chinese emperor's administration gave peacock's tail feathers – with one, two or three eyespots – to signal an employee's position in the hierarchy. In Papua New Guinea, the indigenous peoples attend religious festivals wearing costumes made from feathers, often the brightly coloured plumes of the native birds of paradise. Each clan assigns itself a tree where these birds perform their courtship displays and

A crow devours a child on this relief panel from a Romanesque church.

Till Eulenspiegel, known as 'Owlglass' in English, was the mischievous hero of German popular stories of the 16th century.

Societies for the preservation of birds continue to run campaigns in an effort to put an end to the massacre of barn owls in the countryside.

follows the development of the young birds' plumage. Few birds are killed, however, since the costumes are reused, and become precious heirlooms that are handed down from generation to generation.

Harbingers of doom

Perhaps due to their nocturnal activity, owls have often been associated with the forces of evil. For the Aztecs, the owl was the supernatural spirit that attended the god of the underworld; it was an

In the Caribbean, voodoo rituals still require chickens to be sacrificed.

Don't be fooled by this poster. The swarms of birds in Hitchcock's film *The Birds* (1963) terrified his leading lady, Tippi Hedren...and cinema audiences too!

▼ 'The birdcatcher am I, / and always merry, tra la la! / As the birdcatcher I am known / by young and old throughout the land. / I know how to set decoys / and whistle just like my prey. / So merry and carefree can I be, / knowing all the birds belong to me.' Thus goes Papageno's song at the start of Mozart's opera The Magic Flute (1791). Overtaken by events, he incurs the wrath of the Queen of the Night and must overcome the same pitfalls that beset Prince Tamino on his quest for truth before finding his betrothed, Papagena.

embodiment of the night, the rain and the storm. In Europe, as far back as the Middle Ages, the barn owl was seen as the devil's messenger, terrorizing the inhabitants of rural areas with its hooting. To rid themselves or their cattle of evil spirits, some country folk would catch a barn owl and nail it to the door of their barn. This harmless creature was also caught and nailed to a neighbours door for quite a different purpose...this time to bring bad luck!

Beep-beep! Yet again the roadrunner shakes off Wiley Coyote.

A source of artistic inspiration

The many representations of birds in ancient Egypt, the feathered headdresses of pre-Columbian America and Chinese bird kites all have one thing in common: they combine art and religious ritual. In the West, literature, painting and even the cinema have all drawn on the symbolic inferences associated with birds; thus cruelty may be highlighted by a bird of prey, freedom by a dove, and so on. The songs of birds have also inspired musicians. Beethoven's Pastoral Symphony, for example, features the song of a nightingale played on a flute, as well as the song of a cuckoo played on a clarinet.

LE LOUP ET LA CIGOGNE

In La Fontaine's fable, *The Wolf and the Stork*, the only reward for the stork that extracts a bone from the wolf's throat is not to be eaten.

The stork of popular legend

In Britain, Germany and eastern France, the reputation that storks have of being loyal to their nesting sites has given rise to an ancient legend, according to which storks deliver babies when they return from their travels. Further north, it is said that storks can cause women to conceive simply by pinching their leg, while in the East, it seems all they have to do is look at the lucky mother-to-be!

In the French city of Strasbourg, the image of the stork is everywhere.

In Germany, Moritz spa water was reputed to be able to cure infertile women. The spa put out humourous postcards showing storks delivering babies.

BIRDS

star animals

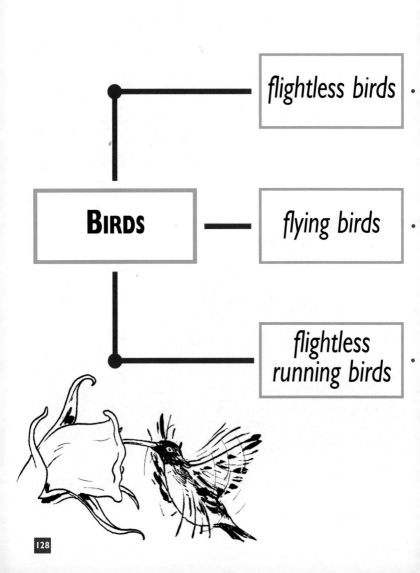

flightless birds ·

BIRDS — flying birds ·

flightless running birds ·

Eagles, buzzards and kites, along with falcons and vultures, form a group of birds of prey which hunt by day.

Like all flightless birds, the emperor penguin has no long feathers (or pennae) at its wingtips.

The albatross, puffin and petrel are all superbly adapted to a marine environment. Unusually for birds, their sense of smell is well developed.

In general, parrots and parakeets are fruit-eaters, although some live on pollen and nectar.

Ostriches live in a harem. The male chooses a site for the nest in which all the females lay their eggs.

The kiwi (a native of New Zealand) hunts for food at night with the aid of its keen sense of smell.

Creative Workshop

*Having studied all of these creatures,
it's time to get creative.*

*All you need are a few odds and ends and a
little ingenuity, and you can incorporate
some of the birds we've seen into
beautiful craft objects.*

*These simple projects will give you further
insight into the world of birds presented in
the pages of this book.*

*An original and simple way to enjoy the wonderful
images of the world of birds.*

Totem boxes

Inspired by Native American totems, these two-tone bird designs are used here to brighten up some simple boxes.
The result is an economical and eye-catching filing system for all your papers.

The stencils
• Photocopy each design twice, enlarging them to the size you require. Glue the four copies on to cardboard leaving a wide margin around each one. Use a Stanley knife to cut around the outline of one copy of each design. Discard the bird and keep the surrounding cardboard. This creates the stencils for the white areas. Cut out the black areas of the other copies. This creates the stencils for the black areas.

Painting the boxes
• If you are using self-assembly boxes, paint on the designs before making the box. Apply spray

mount to the edges of the stencils. Position the stencils for the white areas on the box. Spray on the white paint and remove the stencils. When the white paint has dried, place the other stencils on top of the white shapes and spray them with the black paint.

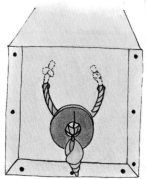

The handles

• Decorate the handles using painted shells, large beads or

even pine cones, using brass wire to attach them.

Materials

• cardboard boxes with cord handles or 1 metre of cord to make your own handles • acrylic spray paint in black and white • 2 sheets of cardboard
• glue • a Stanley knife • spray mount • brass wire and a pair of pliers
• some large coloured beads, shells or pine cones

Beret with bird motif

*B*irds' feathers have been used to decorate hats for centuries. This attractive bird motif is an alternative way of bringing a novel touch to a traditional beret.

Preparing the motifs

• Photocopy the spiral and bird designs four times. They should measure 7 cm and 15 cm in height respectively. Tape the eight photocopies on to iron-on fabric and cut around the edges of the designs.

Attaching the motifs

• Place the four spirals at regular intervals on the beret. Cover them with a damp cloth and stick the motifs to the beret using an iron with the steam setting switched off.

• Position the birds between the spirals and iron them on to the beret in the same way.

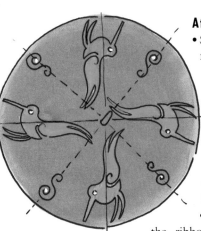

Attaching the beads

• Sew a white bead on to each bird to form its eye. Sew on four others at the centre of each spiral design.

Attaching the ribbon

• Cut a 3-cm length of ribbon, wind it round the tassel of the beret and then fix it in place with superglue.

• Stick the flat bead and the last small bead on top.

• Sew the rest of the ribbon around the beret, overlapping by 1.5 cm at the back.

Materials

• a beret • iron-on fabric in a paler colour than the beret • 70 cm of ribbon
• 9 small white beads • 1 flat bead • an iron • a damp cloth • scissors
• sticky tape • superglue

Bird tray

*H*ere's an idea for brightening up an old wooden tray. The small greedy-looking birds used as part of the design seem ready to peck at the crumbs left over from a hearty breakfast.

Preparing the design

• Photocopy the design, increasing the size according to the measurements of the tray being used.

• Lightly sand the tray. Trace the four bird silhouettes on to the outside of the tray, and trace three birds on to the inside of the tray.

• Fill in the outline of the birds using blue-grey and brown paint.

• Allow the paint to dry, then paint on the detail of the feathers.

Painting the feathers

• Using the tube of gold enamel paint, retrace the outline of the bird designs with a fine even line.

Fill in the black areas of the design with gold paint.

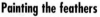

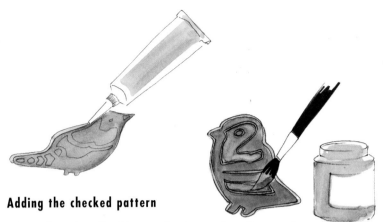

Adding the checked pattern

• Use the tube of gold enamel paint to draw lines at 1-cm intervals along the top edges of the tray. Draw another line along the bottom inside edge of the tray.

• Paint squares along the edges in alternate shades of blue, brown and gold.

• Paint a gold square at each of the four inside corners of the tray.

Materials

• a painted wooden tray • sandpaper • tracing paper • a pencil • a tube of gold enamel paint • brown and blue-grey acrylic paint • a medium paintbrush • a pot of gold paint

Feathered frame

A few feathers and brightly coloured paints are all it takes to transform a simple wooden frame into something that would not look out of place in a cabaret star's dressing room.

Painting the frame

• Paint the frame with a very light acrylic wash, using orange on the top and crimson at the bottom. Ensure that the colours blend into each other gradually.
• Leave to dry and then use sandpaper to accentuate the grain of the wood.

Piercing the frame

• Use a gimlet to make nine holes at regular intervals along the top of the frame.
• Make five more holes along the front of the frame, 1 cm from the top.
• Insert the large feathers into the holes along the top edge of the frame, angling them so that they lean forwards.

Attaching the feathers

• Insert five small feathers into the front of the frame.
• Remove the back of the frame and place five more small feathers behind the glass. Insert a photograph or picture and close the frame.

Adding the handle

• Position the metal handle at the bottom of the frame. Use the gimlet to mark the position for the four wood screws, then screw the handle on.
• Write the name of the photograph on the ticket and slide it into the handle.

Materials

• an unpolished wooden frame • orange and crimson acrylic paint • a medium brush
• sandpaper • a gimlet of the same diameter as the shafts of the feathers • feathers to
match the colour scheme of the photo: here we have used 9 large blue feathers along
the top edge of the frame, and 5 small orange, blue and red feathers • a file drawer
handle and screws

Picture credits

AKG Paris
76b, 80b, 106b, 108b, 109, 110a, 111a, 112a, 112b, 116, 118a, 119a, 119b, 120a, 122b,
124-125, 126, 127b; Cameraphoto: 104; Werner Forman: 107a, 108a, 113b;
Kuzelowsky: 88-89; Joseph Martin: 114a; Gilles Mermet: 115a

BIOS
Jean-Jacques Alcalay: 60b; Henry Ausloos: 16a; Stephan Bonneau: 37a; E. & D. Boyard: 96a;
Denis Bringard: 69a; Régis Cavignaux: 10-11, 48b, 77a, 100; Collection Leber: 72a;
Alain Compost: 30, 35; Tristan Da Cunha: 17a; Dani/Jeske: 2; Dominique Delfino: 22a;
Jean Dufresne: 38b; Edwards/StillPictures: 123b; D. Hubaut/Wildlife: 98a; Michel Denis-Huot: 91;
Frédéric Denhez: 92a; Catherine Deulofeu: 94b; Georges Dif: 103; Xavier Eichaker: 12b, 73b;
Jean-Jacques Etienne: 41a; Patrick Fagot: 88a; André Fatras: 40a; Philippe Feldmann: 31;
Berndt Fischer: 7; R. Ginzburg: 99a; J.L. Gonzales Grande: 48a; Michel Gunther: 57, 58a, 72b, 73a,
76a, 85b, 94a; Kim Heacox/Peter Arnold: 58b; Philippe Henry: 29a; Daniel Heuclin: 6, 32b, 118b;
Hubert/Klein: 11a, 36a, 61a, 70, 98b, 106a; Gérard Lacoumette: 127a; Tristan Lafranchis: 74b, 105,
107b, 110-111; B. Laurier: 8a; Antony Leclerc: 40-41, 141; Jean-Louis Lemoigne: 66a;
Georges Lopez: 62-63, 84a; Berngt Lundberg: 29b, 33a, 54a, 84b; Piotr Malczewski: 92b;
T. Mangelsen/P. Arno: 4; Gilles Martin: 75, 89a, 114-115, 122a, 123a; Jean Mayet : 66-67;
Christian Meyer: 97a; Russel Mittermeier: 68, 120b; Marie de Montesquieu: 74a;
Thierry Montford: 86, 102a; Juan Carlos Munoz: 36-37; J. Newby/W.W.F.: 20b; Laurent Nitsch: 15a;
Jean-François Noblet: 101b; Yves Noto Campanella: 39b; Bruno Pambour: 13; Thierry Petit: 77b,
87a; Alain Pons: 28; Roger Puillandre: 59b; Cyril Ruoso: 12a, 22-23, 45a, 61b, 78a,
80a (Bergerie Nationale), 96-97, 129f; Eduardo Santibanez: 101a; Kevin Schafer/Peter Arnold: 56;
Seitre: 9b, 14a, 18, 19, 23a, 34a, 39a, 59a, 60a, 62a, 63a, 65a, 65b, 79a, 87b, 102-103, 129a,
129e; M. Sewell/P. Arnold: 33b, 129d; Jean-Pierre Sylvestre: 8b; Yvette Tavernier: 117;
Thierry Thomas: 24a, 24b, 25b, 129c; Alain Torterotot: 64b; Frank Vidal: 64a, 90a;
H. Weiherskirch: 99b; W.W.F.-International: 15b; J.L. & F. Ziegler: 81a, 81b, 93a

Cat's Collection: 124a, 125a

D.R.: 32a, 38a, 47a, 87a, 129b

EXPLORER: Bernard Maltaverne: 93b

JACANA
Hermann Brehm: 26-27; Jacques Brun: 51a, 83; John Cancalosi: 55a; Monique Claye: 21a;
Sylvain Cordier: 5, 46, 47b, 49a, 78-79, 85a, 113a; Manfred Danegger: 43, 45b, 52a, 53, 54-55,
82b; Henry Gallais: 82b; Angelo Gandolfi: 50-51; C. Larsen/P.H.R.: 21b; Chlaus Lotscher: 42;
G. Lowell/P.H.R.: 20a; T. Mac Hugh/PHR: 44b; Fritz Polking: 49b; Jean-Philippe Varin: 9a, 52b;
Varin/Visage: 17b, 50a; Tom Walker: 25a; Pat Wild: 26a, 71; Winfried Wisniewski: 44a

KINGFISHER: 10, 16b, 34b, 121

NATURE: Chaumeton/Nature: 95

Front cover:
Nature, D.R. (A), Reille/Nature (B)

Back cover:
Jacana: Sylvain Cordier (A), Winfried Wisniewski (B), Jacques Robert (C), Retherford/P.H.R. (D)

Acknowledgements

The publishers would like to thank all those who have contributed
to the preparation of this book, in particular:

Guy-Claude Agboton, Angie Allison, Sarah Barlow, Rupert Hasterok, Nicolas Lemaire,
Hervé Levano, Mike Mayor, Kha Luan Pham, Marie-Laure Ungemuth

Creative Workshop:
Michèle Forest (p 132-135, p 138-139), Valérie Zuber (p. 136-137)

Translation:
Patricia Clarke, Wendy Lee, Jane Rogoyaska

Illustrations: Franz Rey

Printed in Italy
Eurolitho - Milan
May 1999